LETTERS

ON THE IMPORTANCE OF

THE FEMALE SEX.

Entered at Stationers' Hall.

LETTERS

ON THE IMPORTANCE OF

THE FEMALE SEX:

WITH OBSERVATIONS

ON THEIR MANNERS,

AND ON

EDUCATION.

By Miss HATFIELD,

Author of CAROLINE; or, SHE LIVES IN HOPES;

INSCRIBED BY PERMISSION TO

Her Royal Highness the Princess of Orange.

London:

Printed for the Author, by J. Adlard, Duke-street, Smithfield:
And sold by Vernor and Hood, Poultry.

1803.

PREFACE.

THE subject of the following Letters, having been often discussed by Writers of superior judgment and ability—it may, perhaps, be considered as an intrusion to offer them to the notice of the Public, without the charm of much novelty and originality to recommend them. But although they may not altogether appear with those two powerful attractions, they are not presented as the chimerical ideas of a mere Theorist, who is too frequently discovered to amuse the Public with impracticable schemes; but are the result of reflection, of observation, of some professional experience, and of a tender regard for the happiness and dignity of the Sex. A wish to inculcate ideas of their own importance;—to possess them with that laudable self-esteem which is founded on just and lawful rights;—to incite to a practise of those decencies, flowing from the delicacy of modesty, sensibility, and a well-directed judgment, so beautiful in a female character;—to point out the disadvantages of mental ignorance or neglect—of frivolous pursuits—of dissipation—and of those volatile inconsistencies, which, by a weak indulgence, so

often

often amount to criminal indiscretions—has uniformly directed the Author's pen. She is therefore induced to hope that the accompanying pages will be found to contain some general strictures, worthy the attention of the Fair Sex; but particularly that her attempt to direct the attention of Mothers to a more rational mode of Education for their Daughters, and thus to bring the mental powers of the Female into a nearer competition with those of the opposite sex, will be treated with indulgence.

Men have, indeed, too long thought it an advantage to consign the Fair Sex to ignorance, that, by a monopoly of knowledge, their superiority might be supported.—Women were not permitted to possess just sentiments of their own importance, and of their native dignity—but were encouraged, or controled—were gained or lost—by the most childish, narrow, and degrading methods.

In former times, they even suffered so great a mental degradation, that they were taught sooner to blush at being suspected of sharing the generous gifts of Nature by the use of their understandings, than of offending against the delicacy and honor of their sex. They were indeed sensible of innumerable voids in their minds, which they knew

not

not how to supply, prohibited as they were that Knowledge they so much wanted. In such a state, with their Reason uncultivated, females were exposed to all the dangers of deceit and seduction. To be a machine—an object of passion,—to be lovely, even tho' an idiot in understanding, constituted the esteemed value of the sex. Many illustrious Women, however, by conceiving proper ideas of their own privileges, have assisted to set at liberty that subdued spirit, which custom and prejudice had so long held captive. It became the fashion to impute sensibility to the female character—as its peculiar charm—as the distinguishing trait of a lovely and superior mind; and Education, in acquiescence with an erroneous opinion, unskilfully regardless of the propensities arising from that disposition, has contributed, or rather endeavored, to give it the most unrestrained powers. But, however amiable Sensibility may be, when acting under the direction of the Judgment, as a leading disposition, it proves the most fatal to Female Virtue and Happinefs; and must be considered, by the judicious, an obvious proof of an ill-conducted Education. Their views are now become more extended—a desire of knowledge has animated the female mind; and, eager to possess that which is only to be obtained by a regular pursuit,

they

they have commenced their search of her, though yet uncertain of the right track. In their way, they have gathered such flowers and fruits as the soil presents to them: but, unfortunately mistaking the Genius of Fiction for the Spirit of Truth, they eagerly seize the gifts he has to offer to their acceptance.—It is of such materials that the general class of females form their ideas of life. It is through the false medium of romance, as delineated by the pen of Imagination and Error, that they view human nature and human events. Thus from the School they are conducted to the Circulating Library, whence they receive their qualifications to enter the extensive and difficult seminary of the world. But, may the period soon arrive, in which the Fair Sex will approach nearer the state of perfection, which they are laboring to reach. May they at length, by finding the path of Wisdom and Truth, wholly emerge from the mazes of mental obscurity and error; and, from a dawning of light, be so charmed with the beauteous prospect, that, by an industrious progression, they may enjoy the meridian splendor of intellectual knowledge.— May they be early taught, by Education, to unite Rationality with Feminine Graces—and to know that Happiness is the inseparable companion of Virtue.

London, March 26, 1803.

ON THE IMPORTANCE

OF

THE FEMALE SEX.

LETTER I.

SIR,   *London, June,* 1802.

THE declaration of your motives for preferring a state of Celibacy to that of Marriage, must be received as a testimony that you consider the female sex in a very disadvantageous point of view; and, in order to increase their humiliation, you avow a knowledge of many gentlemen—rational men—who, although sighing for the enjoyment of domestic bliss, yet dare not venture—from impressions similar to your own,

own, to risque their happiness with any— among the present race of females.

You do not confine your disapprobation to existing characters only; but descend to prefer accusations even against Nature herself, whom you charge with having formed that part of her work superficial, vain, in-consequent, without solidity, without character: you are disposed also to aggravate natural imperfections with those peculiar to the day, supposing the fair-sex to be without the necessary reserve of decency, modesty, and discretion; and, from the prevailing mode of their education, wholly unfit for matrimonial faith and domestic confidence.

Such, Sir, are the opinions of those of your

your party, who, remaining ignorant of a finer texture of character, content themselves with more inferior samples—the opinions of men, who, having only experienced the solitary state of celibacy, are necessarily incompetent to decide on the real value of the sex—of men, who must first condescend to exchange the unmanly, unblest, title of Batchelor, for that of the more honorable and dignified—" the husband of one woman,"—before their judgment can be admitted as a substantial evidence against female pretensions to the equal and impartial endowments of Nature.

That the fair-sex in all ages has been a subject against which the acrimony of satire,

satire and the arrows of wit have been directed, the writings of the first and greatest poets testify: that neither the spleen of the one, nor the wantonness of the other, can debase or lessen the intrinsic value of that interesting sex, their unceasing influence sufficiently demonstrates.

As the benign properties of the solar rays dissipate and dispel gross vapours in the material world, so does the presence of women operate in the intellectual. Over the mind of a good and sensible man her power is gentle and prevailing; his councils are assisted by her prudence; the rude vicissitudes of fortune are softened by her sensibility and friendship: no estimate can

can exceed her worth, which the wisest of men declared to be " far above rubies."

The motives that induced, and the circumstances that attended, the creation of the first woman, were strong attestations of her importance, and of the great and momentous part she was to take in the future plan and operations of the world; without her, the purposes for which it was created, must have remained unaccomplished and unfulfilled: for, although Nature appeared to be finished in all her parts, through all the range and variety of animal and vegetable creation, from the most minute and inconsiderable, up to the lordly monarch, by whom they were destined to be governed, and every class of

being

being had received that degree of existence to which it was ordained; yet, notwithstanding the admirable co-operation of a vast part, this beautiful system would have remained incomplete, unorganised, created to no end, if woman, " the last, best gift of Heaven," had not consummated the grand design. In vain, until her appearance, did the unsullied beauties of a new creation glow before the ravished eye, and the most delicate fragrance gratify the sense: in vain did the melodious inhabitants of the airy regions chant their raptures around, or the unclouded azure of an eastern sky display itself in the lofty vault of heaven.

Although thus invested and surrounded,
" Monarch

"Monarch of all he surveyed," unrivalled Lord amidst a world of sweets, the heart of Adam was a prey to anguish—already he had learned the tale of woe. "Who can enjoy alone; or, all enjoying, what contentment find?" said the Casuist, when his Maker condescended to interrogate him on the cause of his discontent. The incompetency of every other blessing discovered the forlorn condition of man, and the necessity there was for the creation of another creature. This necessity established the value of *her* society, for whose single absence the whole mass, already produced and in existence, could not compensate.

In a fairer image of improved Nature,

and of a texture refined from the grosser elements that composed the body of man, the lovely form of woman appeared. The spirit of her mind was also sublimated; every thing that could raise and confer dignity on her person and character assisted at her presentation. Nature was clad in her grandest gala for her reception; she was introduced to the world by the Almighty himself.—" On she came, led by her heavenly Maker." And it was not until her appearance, that, like an all-approving father and judge, he pronounced the paternal benediction: it was then that he blessed his work, and declared it to be good.

By the creation of woman, the great design

design was accomplished—the universal system was harmonised.—Happiness and innocence reigned together: but, unacquainted with the nature or existence of evil—conscious only of good, and imagining that all were of that essence around her—without the advantages of the tradition of fore-fathers to relate, or of ancient records to hand down, Eve was fatally and necessarily ignorant of the rebellious disobedience of the fallen angels, and of their invisible vigilance and combination to accomplish the destruction of the new favorites of Heaven.

In so momentous an event as that which has ever been exclusively imputed to her, neither her virtue nor her prudence ought to be suspected: and there is little reason to doubt that, if the same temptations had been offered to her husband, under the same appearances, but he also would have acquiesced in the commission of this act of disobedience.

Eve's attention was attracted by the manner in which the serpent first made his attack: he had the gift of speech, which she must have observed to be a faculty peculiar to themselves. This appeared an evidence of something super-natural. The wily tempter chose also the form of the serpent to assist his design, as not only in wisdom and sagacity that creature surpassed all others, but his figure was also erect and beautiful; for it was not until the
offended

offended justice of God denounced the curse, that the serpent's crest was humbled to the dust.

During this extraordinary interview it is evident, that Eve felt a full impression of the divine command, which she repeated to the tempter at the time of his solicitations. She told him, they were not to eat of *that* tree.—" And the woman said
" unto the serpent, We may eat of the fruit
" of the trees of the garden, but of the fruit
" of the tree that is in the midst of the gar-
" den ; God said, ye shall not eat of it,
" neither shall ye touch it, lest ye die."
But the serpent opposed her arguments with sophistry and promises.—" He said
" unto the woman, Ye shall not surely die,

" but shall be as gods!"—What an idea to a mortal!—Such an image astonished her!—It was not the gross impulses of greedy appetite that urged her, but a nobler motive that induced her to examine the consequences of the act.—She was to be better, and happier—to exchange a mortal for an angelic nature. Her motive was great, virtuous, irresistible. Might she not also have felt herself awed and inspired with a belief of a divine order?—Upon examination, she found it was to produce a greater good than as mortals they could enjoy: this impression excited a desire to possess that good; and that desire determined her will, and the future destiny of *a-world*.

Numberless

Numberless circumstances have been recorded in ancient history, during intermediate ages, in which female abilities and talents have been displayed in various gradations and extremes, anterior to that grand epoch, in which a woman was so conspicuously chosen to assist in the great work of atonement, in producing the Redeemer.

No age has passed, in whose annals have not been recorded acts of female heroism and greatness—of deeds, in which have been displayed illustrious virtue and magnanimity: deeds which have reflected on that sex the brightest lustre, and strikingly discovered the natural richness of their minds, which, receiving very few advantages

advantages from a narrow system, long laid down and established, for their education, they must either have made efforts to free themselves from the mental shackles with which they were bound, and force themselves into acts worthy a human soul, or continue to drag little better than a torpid existence, in that state to which the meanness of their acquired knowledge seemed to condemn them.

Like a lovely tho' neglected plant, whose active gem bursts spontaneously into life, and expands its beauties, generously yielding a valuable and useful essence around, so have those distinguished females exhibited examples to the world, worthy of admiration, and to be imitated.

      I remain, Sir, &c.

LETTER II.

SIR, *London, July,* 1802.

IT is an indisputable truth, that the art of refining and polishing the manners and taste of society, is exclusively possessed by the fair-sex: and that the further any country advances in, and becomes distinguished for, civilization of sentiment, and elegance of manners, the more the prevalence of female influence is discovered amongst them : yet, it is not to the gentler scenes of life alone that their powers are confined—they have ruled empires and kingdoms with justice and dignity.

Illustrious

Illustrious and multiplied examples have manifested, that the bounteous Author of our common being has, like an impartial father, bestowed upon each of the sexes an equal proportion of the reasoning faculty, which ought gratefully to be employed towards the accomplishment of the original purposes of his divine wisdom. Nevertheless, there are to be found mortifying instances of female degradation; but it exists only in countries that exhibit a darkness of manly intellect, and remarkable for ignorance, rudeness, and barbarity. Here woman falls beneath her native dignity, and suffers a treatment little above the lower orders of creation: yet, notwithstanding this servility, the

weight

weight of bondage, and the toil of slavery, the oppressions of cruelty and of violence, their fine spirits aspire, and act by means too subtle for the gross perceptions of a lordly tyrant, strikingly manifesting, by the practices of all the secret, crafty mazes of cunning, the strong operations of an unenlightened and perverted reason.—Unfortunate children of Nature! whom ignorance, barbarity, and luxury, have alike allotted to wear the galling chains of slavery and low subjection—who are condemned to toil, like the beasts that perish, without understanding—your sighs and tears, while they attest you to be fellow-creatures, fail to establish your claims to mercy and kindness, with the Sons of Humanity, and Christians! Yet,

Yet, not to Africa, nor India's shores—is Cunning, that ape of Wisdom, found to confine her sly and artful empire: the untaught peasantry of every remoter province, even in the lettered regions of Europe, intellectually considered, afford a picture little superior to the unenlightened, sooty inhabitants of a torrid zone.

These are evidences that the human understanding, the enobling faculty of the human race, will, from neglect and abuse, degenerate into low instinctive action; while that property, if cultivated in the brute creation, will make near approaches to a resemblance of reason. Since, then, it is Reason that is the distinguishing cha-
racteristic

racteristic of human superiority over the inferior orders of creation—since that is the light placed within us, to guide us in the excellences of knowledge, to self-acquaintance, and to a certainty of the privileges it affords of advancing our state to a still superior rank;—it is an act of the highest ingratitude to the beneficent Spirit who communicated it, and of neglect of our own happiness, to suffer it to be remissly extinguished, or even to burn dimly, when its improving influence has a power of benefiting mankind, and of gratefully ascending to that fountain of goodness, at whose sacred flame it was first kindled.

Experience has established the pre-eminence

eminence of female worth, in all the social duties of life: the finest sentiments spontaneously arise in their bosoms, as their native soil. In the two noblest affections of the mind—Friendship and Love—they excel. In both, they have given the strongest testimonies of being more sincere, lively, and disinterested, than men.

Acts of kindness and benevolence are so attractive in them, that these performances appear to be, exclusively, the attributes of the sex. To their smiles, the festive scene owes its heightened zest; to their soft attentions, the pining hour of langour and of drooping melancholy, its relief.—Their fortitude and tenderness sustain them, not only in a patient, but willing, endurance of all

all the tedious cares and watchings of a sick-chamber.

These are among the virtues that actuate the female sex; from the aggregate use of which, they become raised into characters of exemplary piety: for, as the Christian Religion enjoins the performance of those acts that benefit, and prohibits the perpetration of others that are injurious, to mankind; the female mind, by those practices and forbearances, is put into such a tone, that, by an exemption from many acts committed without scruple by men, females are not only more likely, but better enabled, to attain an higher degree of perfection than the opposite sex—whose violent and self-ungoverning spirit requires,

sometimes,

sometimes, all the influence of feminine virtues to soften and correct. But, in describing the valuable powers of female capacity, the pen would err in representing the full attainment, as being often accomplished, or even generally aimed at.

It is said, the various occurrences of life furnish many obstacles in attempts at perfection: but, are they insurmountable? Ought not difficulties to be encountered rather with resolution and firmness, and suffered to act as a stimulus to proceed? Would not such attempts then appear to be made in earnest? It is wrong to be discouraged, because a distant object cannot be attained at the out-set, when, by perseverance, nearer advances are made

continually

continually to it; and every step taken in the road to perfection, yields its own and immediate reward.

If in the various branches of Education, appointed by instructors for our study and practice, we not only enjoy their approbation, but ourselves also exquisite pleasure, in conquering those difficulties we find in the way, and become more enamoured, the more we acquire a knowledge of the object of our pursuit, how much greater delight must be produced by a progress in moral virtues, when the mind becomes ennobled, refined, and spiritualized.

This is not an undertaking in which we proceed blindly, uncertain of reward. The

great

great Author of creatures, whose nature his wisdom formed imperfect, that by their own improvement they might merit his favor; and, from the beginning, he ordained to attain perfection by progressive endeavors, has encouraged them to perform with confidence the work he has given them to do, and to proceed, till they become fit to mingle in the throng of Angels before him.

If knowledge be the wing by which the mind is to be raised to the enjoyment of celestial intercourse, our endeavors after it ought to be zealously performed. Who would suffer his soul to be clogged down to earth, when, by divine right, it can aspire

aspire to Deity? Or, by grovelling attachments, be retarded from a serious and timely contemplation of the hope of a happy futurity?

The advantages of these sublime contemplations are not speculative and remote; they even increase our present pleasures and enjoyments: for every fresh illumination the mind acquires, is an immediate communication of new delight.

The untaught soul, that is suffered to lie in rudeness and error, although derived from the same source, has the evidences of its natural powers considerably lessened, compared with that enlightened mind which is enabled to seek into its own expectation. This is the cause whence

whence many illiberal opinions of the opposite sex have suspected female faculties of inferiority: for men, taking the laws of order into their own hands, appeared to form a masculine plot, unfavorable to the advancement, by declaiming against the amiableness, of feminine knowledge, beyond the sphere of domestic life: but although these regulations were no proof of men's wisdom, they added to their importance by the exercise of greater power.

" Wives as they were," were included among the vassals of their lords, whose desire of having undivided dominion, ordained, that the knowledge of females should not exceed the superintendance of an household, or that of making themselves

selves agreeable objects of dalliance, when the condescending lord should be disposed to amuse himself, in hours of relaxation from greater pursuits.

Such were the decrees that endeavored to keep the female mind obscured and confined; and, even in later times, their mental pursuits were so ill directed, that one of their severest satirists declared, he had never met with a woman capable of being consistent twenty-four hours together.

It is very disadvantageous to themselves, hat females are left to form their opinions and judgments from perception only, or from the illusory effects of things upon their senses; while the minds of the opposite sex not only become strengthened and freed from error, but enjoy the full exercise of their faculties, and are furnished with ability to think and reason justly by regular, progressive, and philosophical studies, and are habituated to the beauties of truth and certainty by mathematical demonstration.

Must this imputed difference be placed to Nature's partial and circumscribed endowments of feminine abilities, or to a narrowness of the means made use of in the cultivation of her gifts? Nature has generously done her part; and the powers of the female mind are equal to the highest attainments, as far as those of human are permitted to go, whether they relate to the boundless ranges of science, or in exploring the

the depths of nature and of art, in the most abstruse and difficult researches.

Neither are their bosoms less capable of exercising the firmer and nobler dispositions of courage and resolution—had their country's cause commanded their aid in the council and in the field, the ardor of patriotism and heroic valor would have directed and sustained them there: or, had Religion or Justice called them to the pulpit and the bar—truth, persuasion, and zeal would not less have accompanied, and crowned their efforts.

But the ordinances of superlative Wisdom appointed a sphere for female action, more important and engaging. Society looked to that sex for happiness, for prosperity;

prosperity; duties, the most amiable, indispensable, and arduous—relations the most endearing—cares distinct and separate from those of the opposite sex, beautifully and reciprocally constituting appropriate convenience and variety. The regulations and management of private domestic life communicate their influence to the sphere of public action; and while its good order secures the comforts and happiness of one, it cannot fail to assist and promote the welfare and prosperity of the other.

I remain, Sir, your's, &c.

LETTER

LETTER III.

SIR, *London,* 1802.

WHILE the youth of your sex are devoted to such studies as impart strength and solidity to their mental faculties, the precepts of female education inculcate to her pupils superficial knowledge, and exterior advantages only; such as induce them, at a very early period, to suppose themselves to have been born only to attract the regard and admiration of the opposite sex: even parental conduct contributes to intimate that designation.

Apparently, the primary cause, the grand design, the ruling motive, the ultimate end for which a parent provides, anxiously watches, and educates his daughter, is to secure to her an advantageous settlement: and he thinks his labours abundantly crowned, if she has the happy destiny of sharing the riches of any man that possesses them.

Let felicity or discord reign, beyond the nuptial day he seems to penetrate not. In order to qualify her for this propitious event, a store-house of artillery is opened for her education: the piano-forte, that staple instrument, from which the magic fingers, gliding with unresisted rapidity, produce the most soul-subduing strains, has,

has, unaided, effected innumerable conquests; but when coalesced with the voice Italianized, and the soft languishments of tone and gesture, are considered to vanquish by a *coûp-de-main*. To these qualifications, is added a facile ability to converse in the French and Italian languages; which, with the Ariel movements of a *Parasôt* in the captivating Art of Dancing, gives a brilliant effect to the design.

'Thus, at the age for presentation, a moment often and ardently sighed for, with the auxiliary aids of the mysteries of the toilet, the accomplished pupil becomes irresistibly armed for conquest. Ready she makes her *debût* at the usual places of exhibition, and encounters, *au merveille* the formidable gaze of the *grand monde*; where, darting through the hemisphere of fashion, she draws her satellites around her.

Her captives gaze and adore. The strains of adulatory praise are new and harmonious to her delighted ear. All is enchantment. The lovers, from early impressions, and perhaps some experience of female weakness, not expecting to find a mind in their mistress, think they have only to disclose their own, by swearing that no woman is half so much an angel—in the management of the fan—the display of the hair—the enchanting wave of the plume—or the soft languishment of the eye.

It

It is enough—the charms that had the power to captivate, command attention: and the fan, the curl, the plume, and the eyes, receive each an hour's lesson in the day.—But when the soft tones of adulation begin to relax, and die away, and their intermissions yield no resource— when Converse might elegantly present her claims, and Sentiment preside—what has the vacant mind to offer? Frivolity and affectation supply their place—the spirit languishes, until the lover mercifully recalls his mistress to life by renewed flattery.

But, can rational creatures always live to sense? Can a man for ever gaze upon the melting eye, feed upon the roseate cheek, and languish in the lap of beauty? Or can a combination of exterior charms enchant for ever? These are not the only requisites that are necessary to give security to the most solemn engagement in life—to bonds dissoluble by death only, or, worse than death—dishonor!

The compacts of fashionable life result not from elegant friendship, from sympathetic affection, or from the refinements of moral union: the blaze of their Hymeneal torch soon appears dim—it lighted only the hemisphere of rapture, and suddenly reached its horizon—the vivid glare of vision and gay imagination are obscured by an impenetrable gloom: they

they thought not of the purer beams of Reason, that burn with equal rays, while Passion sleeps.

No matter whether the husband be atheist, gambler, or blockhead—he was wealthy—and was won: to him midnight clubs, the gaming table, and mistresses, by turns, present themselves to dissipate the vaporous atmosphere of wedlock. —The fair-one, no longer diffusing life-giving smiles from an angelic orbit, ungraciously descends in frowns, to be considered as a woman! as a wife! and deserted too!!

Is there no remedy? No means left to regain her sphere?—Yes; numberless are before her, assisted by all the privileges of
a married

a married woman, and the aid of pecuniary power. At the card-table she is distinguished by the brilliancy of her vivacity, and her losses; at routs and balls, in full *eclât* of beauty and splendor, she exhibits her person, and dissipates her nights: here she is assailed by experienced seducers, and again draws rapture from new, but fouler, springs of adulation.—Skilled in the assault he meditates, the artful deceiver exclaims with admiration at the elegant folds of her drapery, the enchanting display of her foot, and the gracefulness of her walk—that the fashionable laugh (just heard across the room) by which the finest set of teeth in the world were displayed, was a triumph

umph of a superior mind over vulgar bashfulness.

Thus trained, unguarded, and attacked, how can a superstructure raised on mere weakness escape the ruin that threatens, and by which it is on all sides exposed?

The Gazettes of the day, taken from the proceedings of the Commons and the House of Lords, present the public with the subsequent state of modern conjugal faith—alarming testimonies of perverted and superficial education, whose frail and showy qualities, while they are received and sanctioned under the universally admired appellation of fashion, involve the unhappy object in all the miseries attendant

ant on a violation of the most sacred moral duties—afford to the candid and discerning observers of human life, painful subjects of serious reflection, and to the censurers of the age, gratification in the exercise of satire's keenest lash.

As the best counteraction to those disorders, all nations have agreed in the necessity of a strict education, which consists in the observance of moral duties.

From the power that education possesses in promoting such an end, it must be considered, in respect to the mind, what culture is to the soil, in which there exists an active principle that spontaneously produces. "Weeds and flowers promiscuously shoot." It is the work of education

cation to extirpate those noisome intruders, that the lovely shoots of virtue should not be injured or destroyed by their noxious influence.

But can the end be obtained without the means? Must not that which is sown in error, be necessarily raised in folly?

It is an opinion universally allowed, that female education was never so much attended to as in the present day. But, notwithstanding the elegancies with which the existing system is adorned, and the delicacy with which it is refined, modern education has already discovered, that it will not generally bear the test of domestic proof—that its consequences are far more injurious to the happiness of society, than the limited

limited systems of preceding times, when the province of female engagements was less extended, and *its* scenes of action were bounded by simplicity; when confined within a narrower sphere, they were presented with fewer temptations to err.

The misconduct of the fair sex is the result of improper tuition: from improper culture, the loveliest flower degenerates, and is thrown away, like a noisome weed.

If then Education produces such important effects upon the human mind—if, like a guardian monitor, ever ready, it has the power to direct in the unequal, varied, and sometimes rugged conditions of life, by pointing out the evils that ought to to be shunned, and the good that might be embraced—if its counsels can admonish to virtue, and deter from guilt—it is of the first importance that females, in particular, should be well instructed in that knowledge which will enable them better to discern and avoid the evils with which they are daily solicited by surrounding temptations.

Too often are they like travellers, encompassed by darkness, in a mistaken path, who, finding no firmness in the basis on which they tread, and obscurely enlightened by a glare of error, follow the faithless guide through a maze of danger, till the trembling mire sinks beneath their feet, and hides them for ever from the rays of truth and virtue.

As

As the body cannot acquire strength and vigor without regular and wholesome exercise, neither can the mind attain sufficient force, unless occupied in the pursuit of such studies as have the power to fortify it. When enervated by frivolity, and directed by caprice, it must remain deficient in solidity, and incapable of conducting itself with the unaffected dignity and regular decorum, so requisite to preserve a footing in honorable life.

Such minds are sensitive, without the power of resistance, yielding to every touch. They are without resolution to defend themselves, or force to combat opinions, however dangerous, when presented in the flowery garb of eloquence. They are, from habitual thought-

thoughtlessness, incapable of discovering the tendency, or of weighing the solidity, of opinion; therefore, it is not to be wondered at, that even Virtue, all-powerful as she is, does not always secure an advocate, nor Vice an opponent. Few efforts are required to amuse and laugh them out of the necessity and loveliness of the one, into a reconciliation with the deformity of the other.

The danger is yet greater that attends the careless levity of the still virtuous, whose untainted minds, although they imagine not the designs they occasion, yet afford hopes to an artful seducer, who, disgusted with common vice, meditates an higher gratification in a new destruction; and, like a regular besieger, impressed with

with an idea of the natural weakness of his object, certain of success, watches all ungarded moments, nor quits, until he obtains, and lays his conquest in ruins.

I am, Sir, your's, &c.

LETTER IV.

SIR,   *London, June 2, 1802.*

VANITY, and a desire of admiration, have been fatal to many among the loveliest of the sex: dispositions that are not exclusively attributes of the female character, but incidentally excited by the effects of their beauty and attractions upon the minds of those beholders susceptible of their powers. Even education itself has so largely contributed to introduce those qualities into the female disposition,

sition, as to cause them to be considered native of their minds.

Were their nobler faculties better cultivated, the fair sex would rise superior to those weaknesses. Not only their inconsiderate volatility would be counteracted by the influence of higher motives and principles of action, but they would be also guarded against the contingent dangers of outward temptations. They would know, that the mere superfices of reserve and formality are not virtues, and have no radical power to protect them, too frequently assumed only, and maintained with impurity of heart.

The genuine feelings of Nature are virtuous, and would rise more pure and unsullied,

unsullied, if they were directed by reason and good sense to a proper knowledge of their use; but flow stronger and less amiable, from ignorant attempts to repel and correct them, and too frequently become an irresistible torrent.

Without the co-operation of rational motives, young females listen, as to an old and hacknied story, when they are told, that the first and chief characteristic—the real and personal dignity—of their sex—consists in Virtue; that a deviation from her precepts blots their name with the foulest disgrace, and expels them, like contaminated members, from the society of the chaste and virtuous.

In vain shall Wisdom inculcate, that

the man who persuades them to dishonor, will, like a successful general, glory in a publication of his victory; that his contempt and desertion will precede that of the world's: no circumstance, however mortifying—no sufferings, however painful—corporeal or mental—are sufficiently powerful to preserve multitudes of the unfortunate among the sex from the ruin that awaits dishonor.

It is only when the sullied soul awakes from its guilty delirium, that prevailing Reason restores Conscience to her duties. It is then that the sudden pang of conviction discovers to the agonized bosom the magnitude of its woes. It is when compelled, yet unfit, to take a review, that the mind would escape from self-contemplation; torments reign within; and without, the world's contumely darts from every eye a deadly poison into a wound already mortal. The unhappy victim, unable to re-gain the sacred path from which she once has strayed, finds its barriers surrounded by those awful frowns, dreadful as the flaming sword that guarded those of Paradise. Condemnation is already passed, and they are for ever closed upon her. From necessity, a forlorn wanderer; she either drags on a wretched existence in the noisome elements of vice; or, driven by despair, and reverence for virtue, fatally raises the self-destroying hand to close the dreadful catastrophe.

Such is daily the fate of that abused and amiable part of the creation, who, although Nature has impartially conferred on them an equal share of reason, are persuaded into a belief of the inconsistency of its properties—are taught to suppose that the exercise of their understanding, by rendering them masculine, would deprive them of all those feminine graces that constitute them so desireable. Desireable as what?—As beings kept mentally blind, to fall more easily into the snares laid for them by their avowed protectors; as dupes to the designs of artifice! Victims at the shrine of voluptuousness! Desirable, from their indifference about possessing a soul superior to the purposes of iniquity and

and dishonor; yet most desirable, from their sensibility, heightened by the refinements of an education, whose system is a co-operation to the purpose of rendering them still more the objects of desire!

Instead of Piety, Virtue, and Modesty, with their lovely train of blushing Graces, those bulwarks of female honor are destroyed in our fashionable schools, and superseded by the modish terms of fascination of manners, sensibility of feeling, susceptibility of impressions: properties that naturally attract those dangers, which it ought to be the business and aim of education to repel.

Such are the defences that are to guard the sex against the dangers by which they are too often surrounded in their passage through life—against the too frequently successful enterprizes of those descriptions of men, who, availing themselves of a persuasive brilliancy, or superior force of intellectual powers, derived from education; the privileges of custom, or a more general acquaintance with life, and a deep knowledge of the mysteries of intrigue, discover an unmanly triumph in supporting the distinguishing title of betrayers and common despoilers of what they deem the weaker sex.

A moderate knowledge of the general plan and dispensations of Nature abundantly discovers, that those creatures which she has left defective of reason, are

are most under the dominion of the passions; and that those among human beings, whose understandings have been the least improved, are most subject to their operations.

The various passions and instinctive impulses that actuate every living creature, were implanted, originally, for the wisest and best purposes; namely, for their respective happiness and preservation. These are materials which it is the work of reason to refine into permanent and active virtues; and thus, like refreshing breezes, while they prevent the mind from becoming stagnated and corrupted by a motionless calm,

calm, they will waft us cheerfully along the hazardous ocean of life.

It is against the rude gusts and storms of passion we have to guard, which, when rising to a hurricane, wreck even the soul, and engulph it in a dreadful abyss. In the divine faculty of reason only, an efficient power can be found to oppose their violence and impetuosity: Reason, by enabling the mind to effect a self-government, corrects the giddy and excessive levity of youth, so disadvantageous to reputation —would render young people in general more amiable and attractive in the estimation of men of sense and honor, by whom they would be considered as rising, not only into the important characters of confidential

confidential wives, and reasonable companions, but also as mothers, qualified to train their tender offspring to the practice of truth and virtue.

But, chiefly, will strengthened reason, fortitude, and resolution, be found necessary in the disconsolate state of widowhood and orphanism? When, by the inexorable hand of Death, bereaved of the protecting arm on which they had so long depended—of that countenance, whose smiles had never been contemplated without pleasure—of the companion, in whom were united the affectionate friend, the kind protector, and the faithful counsellor: in this affecting state, the delicacy and weakness to which education has brought the female mind, become unhappily increased by the corroding pang of sorrows, and render them easy victims to formal combination, or to interested individuals, who, like vultures, hover round to despoil and devour their helpless prey.

The range of human life does not present a picture with deeper touches of woe, than the unpropitious circumstances of such a state. As every day is productive of these events, such means ought to be adopted as appear best calculated to enable the mind to encounter them with reasonable fortitude; such as, while they weaken their power, must also alleviate their distressful consequences.

But

But how destitute must those minds prove themselves to be of these requisite and solid qualities, which have been nurtured in weakness, and matured in dissipation—that are sensible of their existence only, when invited into action by scenes of amusement and frivolity—by scenes, whose perpetual and varied changes are particularly calculated to enervate and destroy the nobler principles of the soul!

If we examine their alternate relief, and take a view of the attractions that invite to the closet's retirement; we shall there discover the worthless, unprofitable pages, over which our vacant females sacrifice many invaluable hours of life, their feelings, and their judgments——whence they derive their tone of thinking, and to what cause may be ascribed a large portion of the inconsistencies that have long misled and discredited the female character; namely, those ephemeral novelties, the offspring of heated imagination and distorted fancy — hourly issuing from the press, to supply the shelves of those pernicious schools—the Circulating Libraries.

As well might it be expected, that vapid froths, and nauseating sweets, produced from poisonous compounds, have power to give bodily health and vigor to the animal functions.

If men judged well, they would perceive,

ceive, that on themselves ultimately fall the consequences of the imperfect education of females. If, on the other hand, they would condescend to discern, that that sex have an equal share of intellect with themselves, they would not only receive from that consideration the sincerest pleasure, but also an immense profit from such a discovery. Family scenes would not be deserted for the gaming-table, clubs and taverns; nor such considerable sums, in consequence, transferred from domestic enjoyment.

Mortifying, indeed, must be the condition of an intelligent woman, whose mind is advanced in superior knowledge, whom the most persuasive measures have won,

won, when she finds herself transplanted from native happiness to a deserted hearth, exchanging the enlightened intercourses of social converse, and soul-illumined faces, for the tedious task of watching, with fixed and vacant look, the glowing embers as they waste, or of counting the solitary movements of her needle, until a midnight hour restores her husband, perhaps in a state of inebriation, or a sullen disposition of reproof for her anxious, though offensive, inquietude.

Thus are women unfairly excluded from those rational enjoyments of mental intercourse—from the field of those enlightening arguments, in which reason is exercised and strengthened—the ground of which

which is declared to be holy, and alone consecrated to masculine dignity, on which woman must not irreverently presume to tread. To be silent, is the imposed duty of her sex.—To listen with wonder and awe at his surpassing knowledge, is one she owes her husband; and although she is not allowed to think for herself, yet she is expected to render to him a full account of her actions. To be presentable as an ornament or appendage to a brilliant establishment, to be able to preside with *eclât* at scenes of festive gaiety and pleasure, are the full estimate of her powers, beyond which no survey is taken.

I remain your's.

LETTER

LETTER V.

SIR, London, July, 1802.

THE peculiar features that characterise the present epoch of female education, manners, and exterior appearance, too largely contribute to support several of the charges exhibited against them by many, and some of their sincerest friends and admirers, amongst the opposite sex. Can Modesty contemplate the most refined assemblies? Can she view the streets of the metropolis, or glance even upon the remotest retreats of humble life, without a conscious a conscious sigh—that her empire is departing? Can the serious or less severe among the females behold those fashionable dishonours of their sex, without suffering the sensible pain of offended delicacy? Can men of sense contemplate them without regret; or even the professed libertine, without surprise? Can the masculine air, the undaunted brow, or the eyes that encounter with triumph those of the astonished beholder, unlovely emblems of fashionable tuition and perverted instructions, fail to produce the most painful considerations in the minds of judicious observers?

If we examine the creed of modern days, consider the tenets of which it is composed,

composed, and trace the prevailing influence that has attended its promulgation, we shall no longer wonder at the consequences that have thence resulted. It directly inculcates, that modesty and virtue are no longer requisite to fulfil the individual and social duties of life—that the swell of passion, too noble to be restrained, ought alone to impel the actions of free and unaccountable beings. For, say these reasoners, since the certainty of a future state has become, at least, questionable; the restraints of religion and stern morality, by controuling the generous spirit of inclination, serve only to interrupt and sour those pleasures and delightful enjoyments with which the present

present life is replenished. Why should the bolder disciples of later discoveries be confined within the narrow maxims of ignorant predecessors, who, pusillanimously yielding to the shackles of restraint, practised their vices in the shades of privacy? Be it the distinguished privilege of enlightened minds to display their crimes and follies to public view!

Is this the age that pretends to and boasts of a clearer knowledge, and of an abler defence of Virtue than any of preceding times? It is an age conspicuously distinguished for deserting her standards, and surrounding the ensigns of Vice—sentiment and chastity are driven from the female bosom, in which immorality

rality and voluptuousness triumph. The beautiful robe, with which Modesty was wont to attire her votaries, in whose elegant train the Graces played, is thrown off with their garments; and, in their deficiency for the purposes of decency, the perverted mind unveils its latent impurities.

Under such temptations, men cannot be considered as seducers of the sex, whom they are invited to approach by irresistible solicitation. Return then, primitive Simplicity, return!—when Religion and Modesty were the bulwarks of Virtue and Innocence—when the terrors of Disgrace veiled the acts of Vice and of Iniquity.

It

It is a truth worthy of being regretted, that the British fair, by continually sacrificing their native to foreign manners, have considerably lessened their claim to that homage formerly paid them for the superior worth of their own: they have unwisely exchanged pure sterling ore for a composition of base and counterfeit metal, which, possessing in itself no intrinsic value, must prove their lightness upon the beam, in the balance of which they used to preponderate.

The look of confidence less captivates than the retiring eye. The cheek, pallid and faded by art and midnight revels, is far less enchanting than Nature's roseate bloom. The bosom, open to profane

and

and vulgar gaze, excites offences, and loses every charm that the pure veil of modesty alone can heighten. The deep-toned voice and hoarse loud laugh fall not half so sweet upon the sense as the dimpled smile and softened accent.

As the female sex is invested with the power of giving a form and colouring to the manners of the age, as well as with the important charge of forming also the plastic mind of infancy, whose embryo thoughts are created, obedient to the images first presented to their rising apprehension; what can be expected from the management of our present matrons, and from the future offspring, to whom their example may be transmitted.

In

In the present day, the treatment of youth may be very justly compared to the unskilful attempts of empyrics on the body; for, as well as physical, there are also mental quacks, who, never having regularly studied the anatomy of either the body or the mind, try a variety of experiments upon their unfortunate patients: and, as the ignorance of the former sends innumerable victims to the grave, so does the inexperience of the latter obscure or destroy those powers of the mind, which a more skilful management might have raised to great and useful characters.

Multifarious are the forms adopted for bringing forward the minds of the rising gene-

generation: but the propriety and superiority of their respective claims cannot be truly determined, until their effects become established and irremediable. The capricious taste of a directing principal must give to the world a future member.*

Among the innumerable seminaries open for the reception of young ladies, not only about the metropolis, but also throughout the kingdom at large, may be found many Governesses, who are either unqualified, or above presiding at the head of their establishments: like Monarchs, they govern their juvenile subjects by the appointment of a Premier, re-

---

* These observations are by no means to be considered as general; as there are to be found most exemplary exceptions.

maining themselves solicitous for little more than the ways and means of supporting the dignity and importance of their dominion.

Oppressed with fatigue, and uninterested in the event, regardless of any thing beyond the returns of remuneration, the Sub-governess gets through the routine of business, without considering that the mind of her pupil may be less correct, less lovely, at the close of the day, than the leaf she taught to spring from the embroidered canvass. She aims at exterior graces; and, aided by mechanical means, applies her own ideas of personal elegance to torture the lovely forms under her power; ignorant, or not considering, that, whether of posture, or of manners, true grace is unaffected; not to be created by outward contortions—emanating from the mind, and the result or offspring of the sentiments and feelings, inherent there.

The present regulation of many public schools is unpropitious to the advancement of morality, and the preservation of unsullied delicacy. The purest cherub is in danger from artful associates, among whom many have issued from those *barriers*, matured in all the variety of falsehood, treachery, and intrigue.

Within these abodes is often found, concentred in one individual, every vice, the most alarming to a tender parent. Women, who, driven from their native

soil

soil by the most flagrant practices, and whose education is of the lowest order, are indiscriminately admitted into schools, as indispensable auxiliaries, in the character of French Teachers, though their personal indelicacy, frivolous, if not dangerous, conversation, and levity of manners, ought to exclude them from every establishment appropriated to the education of youth.

The arduous and important task of giving a proper bias to the female mind— of inculcating precepts, and manifesting examples, ought not to be entrusted to any but those who have given the strongest proofs of religious and moral virtues—and who, to a knowledge of the various affections of the human heart, add judgment and experience to direct its pursuits.

To watch with a tender interest the progress of her pupils, and with a discriminating and ever vigilant eye to direct the assisting hand of her subordinates, is the indispensable duty of the superior of a school. What then must be said of those establishments, daily forming under public patronage, for the instruction of female youth, by women, not only of impeachable, but even of desperate, characters!

A Governess, who, in addition to her knowledge, is also impressed with the various duties incumbent upon her station—who has equally in view the ultimate good of an individual, and of society, will previously devote her attention to the forming of an useful and amiable character, by exciting the best dispositions, and giving an ascendant in the heart to truth, compassion, benevolence—with their fair companions, the social virtues, and relative affections.—She will consider the art that unfolds their duty and happiness as pre-eminent above all others; and that, by advancing and cultivating the principal power of their mind—Reason—she furnishes them with a constant and unerring guide to direct and regulate their actions.

Neglectful of these considerations and properties, other instructors confine their labors

labors and views, to light up and enforce the energies of the imagination and memory: they endeavor to form a brilliant, rather than an amiable, character; leave unrestrained and ungoverned passions to take the lead of reason, while the neglected heart remains occupied by falsehood, cruelty, dissimulation, and craftiness. A volubility of tongue, obstinacy of argument, a fervid and emboldened look, frequently distinguish pupils of this discipline.

It appears to be the peculiar and favorite aim of fashionable tuition, to divest her disciples of a certain ensign of vulgarity—by some called bashfulness—denominated

minated in the old English school—modesty: more fashionably stiled, by our unblushing neighbors, *mauvaise-honte.*—This lovely characteristic of a conscious mind, acting upon the fine and delicate organs of sensibility, being dismissed in the outset of life, the pupil becomes prepared to encounter every incident: she may enter any circle, listen to any tale or conversation with *sang-froid* and an undisturbed countenance.

The attainment of this accomplishment derives great acceleration from the free methods adopted by the most fashionable dancing-masters, who, in their lessons to young ladies, frequently produce scenes from which genuine Modesty cannot fail to turn averted; while the present licentious stile of female attire conduces not a little to heighten and even to promote these offences.

I remain, &c.

LETTER

LETTER VI.

Sir,   *London, August* 10, 1802.

I AM induced to believe, that education is less difficult in its application than it is generally supposed to be; the greatest impediments and difficulties that accompany it, arising either from ignorance on the part of the instructor, or from the untimely interference of parents or friends. Volumes have been, are, and will be, written, and a variety of experiments tried, which serve only to involve the

subject

subject in greater difficulties, many general rules may be given; particular ones can only be exercised as incidents and characters render them necessary. But whatever may be the rank, condition, or circumstances of the pupil, there is one indispensable and unerring truth, that ought never to be effaced from the mind of a conscientious teacher.

Since the great Author of our common being has not kept from us the knowledge and power of contemplating the reason and end of our existence—as Revelation has been permitted to signify the former; and as every moment conveys to us, upon its wings, indubitable proofs of the latter; namely, the mortality of our material nature;

nature; which, although some, from the casual superiority of its constitutional parts, may exist to a longer duration, yet must inevitably be dissolved; we must necessarily extend our views, and act agreeably to the inference, that to create, for no other purpose than to destroy, would be irreconcileable with our ideas of divine wisdom and goodness.

This conclusion will impress upon the instructor's mind, a strong consideration of the importance of her work. She will reflect, that the beautiful casket, committed to her care and embellishing, was created subservient only to the purpose of receiving a spark of divinity, which no mortal power is able to extinguish;

guish; but how it is to burn, whether dimly or clearly—whether in the gross vapours of Vice, or in the pure flame of Virtue, lies much in the power of those to whose management it is committed. In either state, it is immortal.

Education, however, can never totally efface the original stamp of Nature. A good one will amend a subject naturally ill-disposed; but cannot raise it to an equal perfection with another, whose disposition, naturally amiable, has been acted upon by the same means. A mind, sordid by nature, although education and fortune have conspired to effect a favorable alteration, will never perform a liberal act with the motives or sensations of one, who,

who, destitute of those fortuitous advantages, discovers from secret feelings alone a native benevolence of heart. Nor does a temper, naturally inclined to suspicion and treachery, prove so faithful in friendship, as when Nature acts upon the sensible springs of kindness and affection, although with the disadvantage of having been tutored by opposite maxims.

Too often Nature's finest works are injured by unskilful management; and her least amiable, are, by judicious culture, rendered tolerable, and, sometimes, valuable, members of society.

Although the amiable dispositions naturally excite regard and love, yet there is no merit in possessing what is merely constitutional;

stitutional; neither are they sufficient. Agreeable dispositions may arise from a happy organization of body, wholly independent of the will.

To learn moral goodness as an art—to study its rules, reasons, motives, tendency, and attributes—to possess resolution to struggle with and subdue the bad dispositions—to persevere in cultivating the best—to regulate and counterpoise the various affections and passions of the mind—to discharge faithfully and cheerfully the relative duties of life, are exercises indispensably necessary to constitute a virtuous character.

Since virtue is the duty, as well as the only source of happiness to individuals, it

is

is an error to reward youth for the practice of it: by such methods, the purity of the motive is in danger of being lost in selfishness. That duty becomes a venal one, which is performed from the promise and expectation of reward. Virtue in herself ought not only to be represented amiable, beneficent, and dignified, but it should also be inculcated, that an obedient fulfilment of her commands insures the highest felicity to her disciples.

The order of divine government daily demonstrates, in its dispensations to mankind, no other reward in this life for the most virtuous conduct, than that which immediately results from self-contemplation and conscious rectitude; wisely deferring

ferring the recompence of finite goodness —to an infinite retribution.

It is a declared opinion among many ladies of high rank, that subordination has been lessened, since the common class of people received the benefit of instruction. When a lady expresses a preference to illiterate servants, does she not discover a tincture of feudal prejudices? Are not all the stations of life subordinate?

The whole economy of Nature is a system of subordination; the lower classes of society form the solid basis of a community, as essentially necessary to its support and duration, as are its most polished parts and superfices. Do the most exalted feel themselves injured by employing a well-informed well-informed subordinate? As well may it be supposed, that monarchs find it inconvenient; and that their first ministers are rendered less desirable, and less calculated for their purposes, by having received a liberal education.

It is very improbable that a liberal-minded superior can be incommoded, merely because a servant is properly instructed, whose duties are better and more clearly understood by an ability to read the Scriptures, and such other books as their leisure moments allow them to peruse, which at once instruct and assist them in maintaining a decent and honest deportment, through that humble, dependent, yet

yet useful, walk of life, to which Providence has destined them.

Nevertheless, by misapplication, these advantages have been frequently converted into serious evils. We have daily proofs exhibited of the mischiefs attendant upon the presumption of the lower orders of society, from their over-leaping the bounds by which they ought to be limited, and encroaching upon certain branches of education, belonging exclusively to ladies of rank and fortune.

Hence, the daughters of persons, even below the class of common mechanics, are made members of boarding-schools, and instructed in such polite accomplishments, as cause them afterwards to blush at, and contemplate with disdain, their origin and paternal roof. Fingers, which improperly have been taught to run over the ivory keys of a piano-forte, to guide the pencil, and to delineate a figure in embroidery, become very unfit for the hardy, yet more useful, work, of giving a polished neatness to the necessary articles of a plain and decent household.

In marriage, these young people recoil with contempt from the proposals of an equal; they delusively aspire to men of fortune and condition. These fleeting hopes vanishing in disappointment, they at length seize upon the shadow. When dishonorable terms, and desertion, have
driven

driven these unfortunate objects into the public streets, and plunged them into scenes of complicated sufferings and guilt for the support of a miserable existence; it is then that the unhappy consequences of their mistaken and ill-judged education become manifested.

The valuable knowledge which these orders of society would derive from being well taught in reading, writing, arithmetic, and needle-work, would better enable them to maintain, not only a more virtuous, but also a more useful, character in their respective stations. All supernumerary accomplishments, except where genius discovers peculiar tendencies, serve to open a field of temptation, incompatible with

with the morality and ultimate happiness of humble individuals.

Although dancing be frequently included in their education, it is an acquirement practically hurtful to their morals. If the academies, daily advertised for this gay accomplishment, with which the metropolis abounds, were well investigated; they would be found to be hot-beds, productive, not only of dangerous indiscretions, but sometimes of the most fatal vices.

In addition to tuition, is held out the allurement of regular, and well-attended assemblies; where indiscriminately, meet the humble, obscure, inexperienced, female, and the openly professed wanton,

wanton, attired and sparkling in all the gaudy trappings of tinselled finery.

To these rendezvous resort clerks from counting-houses, journeymen, and the apprentices of shopkeepers—smiles, gaiety, conviviality, dress and ornament prevail, and beguile—appointments are made for succeeding evenings, intrigues ensue, expences are profusely incurred, and not only the unwary youth becomes a prey to female designs, but he also has his triumph over Simplicity and Virtue. Unable to supply the prodigal demands of the desperate career into which he has incautiously plunged, the title of the gay and assiduous gallant becomes darkened into that of the unhappy victim;

victim; his faith, his integrity, his honesty fall sacrifices, in the commission of those flagrant acts, which at length yield him up to the offended laws of his country.

Your's, &c.

LETTER

LETTER VI.

Sir,   *London, September* 20, 1802.

ALTHOUGH private tuition offers fewer risques, and would, under judicious arrangements, almost exclude every other, it is at present open to some exceptions.

This mode of education was formerly confined to families of distinction and fortune, who, judging it expedient not to expose their offspring to the dangers of public seminaries, secured to them the advantages of paternal protection, by engaging the exclusive and undivided cares of a lady, whose regular matured education, and

and suavity of manners, should intitle her, not only to the confidence and friendship of her patrons, but also to the uncontroled government and respectful regards of her pupils; an attention to whose person and manners, their literary studies, useful and ornamental works, with an intermediate inspection of the various accomplishments, taught by masters, limited her obligation.

A Governess, in those days, had her hours of ease and enjoyment—her happiness and affections were interwoven with the work in which she was employed. Under such regulations, and relative dispositions, private instruction was the plan of wisdom.

But now it presents a different aspect: mothers are become the ostensible Governesses of their daughters; although very few can be found among them, who, either from the extremes of maternal softness or severity, an irritability and capriciousness of mind, arising from dissipation, or from inferior knowledge, are calculated for the philosophical patience and researches of education.

In order that ladies may free themselves from the drudgery of actual employment, they engage very young assistants, at low salaries, whose youth and inexperience prevent them possessing that information, and those impressive manners, so essentially necessary to secure the respect and

and attention of her pupils, either for her counsels or her person. Yet, that this assistant may be able to save the expences of masters, she is expected to be an epitome of knowledge: she is to know, and to communicate, the various branches of polite instruction; the French and Italian languages, music, drawing, painting, geography, astronomy, dancing, writing, arithmetic, needle-work, &c.—parts of education which require half the life of an individual to attain a professional knowledge of.

From the numerous duties incumbent upon her employment, the mind of a Governess is ever in a state of lassitude and anxiety; and she wears out her life under the complicated burthen of fatigue, cold treatment, and disrespectful neglect.

Confined within little less than monastic seclusion, a Governess finds herself a being without an equal associate; considered too humble for her patrons; superior to servants, whose state is rendered enviable from mutual intercourse; tired with the noise of her froward pupils, over whom she has no power—she flies to solitude, as the only good her station has to afford her.

The official authority of a Governess ought not to be questioned, unless unduly exercised; and ought never to be disputed in the presence of her pupils.

There are also particular circumtances in that engagement, which should exclude her from such treatment as might cause her to feel herself a dependant. From the moment she is made sensible of subordinate indifference, her power, her inclinations, her endeavors, will relax; and, being induced to act from the principles of interest only, she will be deprived of the pleasures arising from the performance of voluntary and willing duties.

Thus, from the mortifications inseparable—the duties multiplied—and the treatment incidental—that condition, once the most respectable in the range of female dependent states, is now the least desireable,

able, and ceases to be the profession of a gentlewoman.

Whatever may be the system adopted for education, there cannot be any advance made in it without the assistance of health; it is therefore highly incumbent on those, to whose care young people are committed, to use every means to secure so valuable and indispensable blessing.

Health is too often thrown away in thoughtless negligence, foolish experiments, and imprudent indulgences. The hand-maids that administer to her, are muscular exercises, regularity, temperance, and cheerfulness. The sunk and languid eye may excite pity and commiseration; but

but it is the sparkling grace of health that invites to love.

Nothing is more injurious to this happy system in children, than too early an application to study, whence often proceed, not only a disgust of learning, but sometimes also a confirmed stupidity. The flowers and fruits that are raised by the anticipating culture of the hot-bed, have neither so lasting a bloom, nor yield so fine a flavor, as those that are suffered to attain a regular and natural maturity. The dawnings of reason ought rather to be watched, and made use of, as they arise.

In the first stages of infancy, Nature has much to do; on the performance of which depend the future health and grace of the body. The mind likewise has various objects and wonderful scenes to observe, which afford it better materials for mental exercises; more useful employment than the sickening toils of literary labor: oral instructions are better calculated for children, as they present knowledge in a form more lively, simple, and easy, than that which is acquired from too early an attention to the book, as the extreme, and, sometimes, ungovernable impatience expressed by the pupil, too often, though injudiciously, produces severity on the part of the teacher.

Yet how many parents are there who boast to their friends, at what an early age

age their children are able to recite verses from the most difficult authors, and select passages from the Scriptures. Culpable, pedantic ambition! gratified by cruelty, and the exercise of coercive means; when the young scholar is unnaturally forced to a recollection of words, to which its tender imagination is yet incapable of affixing an image.

To form a just and perfect articulation; to seize with judgment well-timed occasions—sensibly to correct, with gentle firmness, the wayward humors and passions of infancy—to temper the mind, yet soft and plastic, to self-government, mildness, affability, tenderness, and humility, ought at all times to precede scholastic tuition.

As it is the dispositions that form the future personal character, an attention to them is an important part in the task of training an infant's mind: a neglect of this particular has too frequently confirmed how much they constitute the general happiness of the individual. But, to be brilliant and superficial, rather than amiable and virtuous; to be fashionable, rather than good; are the favorite and prevailing attainments of the present day.

Although the age of five years be yet tender, the mind has then begun to survey itself, to arrange its ideas, and to compare them with exterior things—to possess a consciousness of existence—of self-importance; and to be sensible of its dependenpendencies upon others. At that age, the mind is capable of receiving strong impressions; of drawing inferences of its own conduct, and of understanding the dispositions of those towards it, to whom it stands in subjection.

As this state of the mind is too valuable to be neglected, it forms a period at which education might be commenced with propriety and advantage. Children, who have been accustomed to hear the excellencies of learning and knowledge applauded, will not only willingly yield, but also solicit, instruction as the most pleasing employment, if it has been properly represented as the greatest promoter and reward of goodness, instead of being imposed

posed as a task and punishment of naughtiness.

When the reason and dispositions of children have been judiciously prepared; future good regulations, applied with judgment, will exclude the necessity of particular correction: for, as reason is the faculty by which the human species is distinguished, it is by that they must be governed and instructed.

Rational minds yield and expand beneath the genial influence of kindness; but, like the countryman who folded his garments closer about him against the rude attacks of Boreas, in his contest with the Sun, contract, or revolt against
the

the offensive and ignorant attempts of violence.

Such books are best adapted to the tender years of childhood, which are distinguished for their simplicity and easy meanings, whose import will strengthen the powers of their reason; and, while enlivening, will neither mislead nor inflame their imagination: the use of such books, with that variety produced from the exercise of the needle, are sufficient to occupy a considerable interval.

It is the opinion of a celebrated author, that Nature and Reason are insufficient to teach the Being of a God. Nature and Reason, however, fail not to suggest something little inferior, if at all, to that

that truth. They secretly intimate a dependence on some pre-existent superior cause, and, without their being able to affix any certain ideas of creative power, are sufficient to impel an enquiry, of, " How came I thus?—How here?"

How frequently are these interesting little creatures induced to propose questions, that are unfettered by prejudice, unsophisticated by scholastic lore, pure ideas of something new, resulting from the increase of their perceptive powers, and the dawnings of reason: questions which often perplex the understandings of those to whom the application is directed, whose answers are, in general, either too learned,

learned, or too ambiguous, for the comprehension of children.

When these young querists begin to discover theological curiosity, it might be sufficient to inform them, that they were made by, and are dependent on, are watched and governed by, a great and good Power, who, although he be invisible, is yet every where present: that he is the friend and protector of the good and virtuous; the enemy and punisher of the disobedient and wicked.

Inquiries of this nature will precede the age of seven years, at which time the spirits become less volatile, and the understanding begins to acquire a degree of rational solidity: in such a state of mind,

it

it would be proper to make children acquainted with the duty and necessity of prayer; not as it is daily exercised—in cold repetitions—while every attitude expresses impatience and ignorance of the gracious privilege, but pronounced with the solemn articulation and serious deportment becoming so aweful an employment.

From this age, an interval of three years would be very advantageously employed, by introducing the elements of English and French Grammar; the outlines of Geography—the latter as preparatory to a future knowledge of Chronology and History.

In addition to these branches, the art of writing

writing ought to be elegantly taught, joined to a knowledge of arithmetic; a science most useful and valuable, not only in particular concerns, but as it greatly exercises and strengthens the memory: and, more generally, as it relates to, and considerably facilitates, an acquaintance with other sciences, which cannot be well and easily acquired without its assistance.

I am, Sir, &c.

LETTER

LETTER VIII.

SIR, *London, Sept. — 1802.*

GIRLS of strong powers, and lively dispositions, who have been well instructed from the age of five years, will, at that of ten, have acquired, at least, an equal share of knowledge with those children who have been labouring at the oar two or three years in advance. As at this age strong marks of future character will appear, the most vigilant care should be employed, to confirm a regard and habit of Truth; a faculty so indispensably necessary to establish their future reputation

tation and happiness in the world, that the closest investigation should follow every suspicion of a departure from it.

Crafty girls frequently possess the art of refining falsehoods into equivocations, while all the spirit and intention of guilt remain. Sometimes, indeed, when timid dispositions are under severe government, falsehood will arise from fear; as when insignificant accidents, and trivial offences, by causing a dread of unmerited chastisement, not only estrange the affections, but give birth to one of the meanest and most mischievous in the catalogue of human vices—a vice, which no power can banish, when once the mind has established a reconciliation to the practice of it.

False-

Falsehood is a propensity which degrades reputation, and stains the name of the individual with proverbial disgrace: yet base and contemptible as this vice is generally considered, it is too often found ignobly to prevail among females of distinguished rank and fashion.

As we are not only sensible and rational, but also religious creatures, recourse must be had to the doctrines of Christianity, which are laid open in the most simple and intelligent manner, illustrated by example, and sanctioned by practice.

When reason, assisted by the aids of religion, has formed the mind to virtue, education may then embellish her work, consistently with taste and condition. But, as it is not expected, that young ladies of birth and fortune are intended to be musicians and opera-dancers; or that they should enter the lists of competition against a BILLINGTON or a PARISÔT: they ought to make suitable advances in such studies as are calculated to promote their true happiness and interest, before they devote too much time and attention to the elegant, but subordinate, embellishments of music and dancing.

And as the lapse of every departing moment lessens the duration of our, at most, short existence, upon the proper employment of which depend our future hopes; and as Idleness, with her train of slothful associates, never fails to produce

produce a rust upon the principles of action, and to canker the highest faculties of the soul; the most discriminating attention should be used in selecting employment and amusements for the female mind, at once intelligent, graceful, and profitable, and serving to set off the lustre of the moral virtues.

Of all the employments to which the mind devotes itself, literature certainly claims the pre-eminence; its diffusive powers not only afford the most delightful variety, but it also improves the judgment and the heart.

From books are derived an antidote to that prevailing malady—the tediousness of time:

time: in the choice of authors, a preference ought to be given to those who are more distinguished for good sense than learned difficulties; who lead to practice rather than to speculation; and who, by faithfully describing the beauties and properties of Nature, communicate a just knowledge of her laws.

By an attention to these studies, young people are better enabled to discover the various perfections of the Author of Nature: their minds are awakened to the purest affections, and inspired with just sentiments of his divine character and attributes. These contemplations also unfetter the mind, and lift it above those absurd

absurd opinions, and superstitious fears, that arise from a narrow and partial acquaintance with his works.

There is not any branch of female education more intitled to distinction, or that is more amiable in its importance, than the use of the needle. The range and utility of this little implement of industry, are almost unlimited. Innumerable things, which relate either to neatness or to elegance, cannot be effected without its assistance.

Whether the needle be viewed subservient to domestic purposes, in the hands of an housewife; or in the tasteful ones of the scientific LINWOOD, as a

rival

rival to the pencil's richest efforts, in displaying the most exuberant fancy, it equally demands our approbation.

The needle is able to depict Nature herself, however majestic or minute her form, in the justest proportions and most faithful colours.

This employment is also desirable from the calmness, tranquillity, and self-possession, which the mind enjoys, while devoted to its purposes; dispositions unknown to, and unfelt by, vacant wanderers, who, disdaining and flying from the stationary seat of industry, flutter from room to room—from the book, ill-chosen and unprofitable—to the jingle of the piano forte—without enjoying either the desirable state of a well-regulated hour, or affording a single testimony of possessing rational and useful knowledge.

Yet variously beautiful as are the productions of the needle, it is, nevertheless, nearly exploded, by fashionable mothers, in their system of education for their daughters.

They indeed declare an opinion, " that it may be necessary for girls to know how to stitch a wrist-band, work a button-hole, or sew a seam; but, for occupying a larger portion of time, there are higher parts of knowledge, more worthy the attention of those who wish to enter into life with figure and *éclát.*"

From

From such opinions result the sacrifice of valuable days, to the acquiring a brilliant execution on musical instruments, or the ability to languish in the soft movement of an Italian *ariette*—to the desire of being flattered, known, talked of, in the *grand monde*—and at length of shining emblazoned on the lists of Fashion and Fame.

The pencil has a high claim to consideration, not only as it is necessary to assist in the elegancies of the needle, but from its delightful, sublime, and independent properties.

Whether the pencil be employed in depicting the glowing beauties and the lovely tints of the variegated flower; the luxuriant and mingled shades of the richly enamelled landscape; or in pourtraying the sensibilities, and various passions, as they prevail in the soul-illumined face;—its powers are equally great, and worthy of the highest cultivation.

Less generally so is the science of Music, whose seductive powers, particularly at the present period, convert her votaries into slaves.

Although music assists to ameliorate and harmonize the human mind, it is necessary to restrain its use within the limits of temperance. When music is suffered to be indulged with passion, it becomes a
fasci-

fascinating encroacher: by degrees it delights, and at length, like an enchantress, it seizes upon the nobler faculties of the soul, to the exclusion of every rival consideration.

There are particular tones, in certain musical compositions, which, by acting with little less than magic force upon the senses, sometimes make temptations irresistable.

The operations of this charming science are delusive; and the effects it produces, are frequently those either of oppressive lassitude, or of extravagant agitation. Nevertheless, as an ornamental part, music cannot be excluded from a polite and accomplished education: it also becomes one of the most desirable, and delightful, when under the direction and controul of judgment.

Nor is it less necessary to perform well, and with taste; both which may be acquired, without making it the business of life, which it was designed only to relieve, by acting subservient to private, social, or religious purposes.

A general acquaintance with the various branches of natural history, is to be recommended, as being particularly calculated to enlarge the *capacity* of the mind. By studying Nature in all the wonderful economy of her properties, relations and laws,

laws, as they respect the animal, the mineral and the vegetable worlds, we become better acquainted with the dignity and superiority of human nature.

Such a knowledge of all created things will also better enable us to treat them with moderation, and without abuse; and while we are permitted to make them subservient to all the comforts and elegancies of life, we cannot fail to accompany our manifold enjoyments with gratitude to the bounteous Author and Bestower of them.

By a habit of contemplating the beauty, and just arrangements which prevail through the several gradations of created existence, the sympathizing soul receives impressions of a kindred order; and while curiosity is gratified with a rich and boundless variety, not only the taste acquires refinement, and the judgment discrimination, but also method and strength.

It is from an observation and knowledge of the works of Nature that arise the purest sentiments of devotion, a rational homage, and a lively adoration for the Divine Creative Power.

Nature is a field of such an illimitable extent, that, to attain a full discovery and knowledge of its properties, will engage and reward the indefatigable labors, not only of the present, but also of future ages.

Whether

Whether we view it in its common and daily appearances; or, by descending into the depths and caverns of the earth, explore and examine its inexhaustible store-houses of secret treasures—whether, in wandering over its surface, we survey the beautiful variety of the vegetable world—of trees, plants, flowers and fruits; or consider the degrees and variety of animal life, in the exquisite beauty of the feathered creation—the ſtrength, proportion, sagacity, and usefulness of the quadruped—or the delicate, yet perfect, organization of the minutest insect—we shall still have to extend our admiration

tion to the wonders of the ocean, and to the mysterious laws which govern the inhabitants that replenish that world of waters.

These observations strike with awe the breast of the most insensible, at the grandeur that is every where displayed. The most enlarged capacity becomes filled with astonishment and rapture at the wonders exhibited around. It is in contemplating the greatness and harmony of Nature, that the heart is animated with love and adoration of the Supreme Being; and the same heavenly beams of truth that lead the wavering and the doubtful mind on to certainty and demonstration, drive infidelity

infidelity to the caverns of despair, and disarm the daring atheist of his impious weapons.

I remain, &c.

LETTER IX.

SIR, *London, Oct. —* 1802.

It is one of the considerations that gives the present enlarged plan of Female Education a superiority over the old and contracted one of preceding times, that Geography has become one of its distinguishing branches. This science teaches, by artificial means, to see and to compare, at one view, the magnitude, form, and relative situations, of every discovered part of the terraqueous globe. By the help

help of the artificial sphere, a judicious instructor will find little difficulty in giving her pupils clear and rational notions of the natural revolutions of the earth; whence proceed the regular changes of seasons—the different temperature of climate—and the vicissitudes of day and night, light and darkness.

When opportunities and circumstances permit it, after young ladies have acquired a competent knowledge of Geography and the use of the Terrestrial Globe, they are well prepared for learning the elementary parts of Astronomy, and the easier problems of the Celestial Sphere.

Astronomy is a science that greatly
expands

expands the mind, and enables it to form the most sublime conceptions: a capacity that is able to trace the mazes of a country-dance, or to imagine the descriptions of the perplexing difficulties, attending the irregular and intricate adventures of the heroines of modern romances, will, without difficulty, and with considerably greater advantage to themselves, be taught also to conceive the structure of the solar system, and the situations, periodical revolutions, and other circumstances belonging to the heavenly bodies.

As, while teaching Geography, a skilful instructor accompanies the mechanical part of her lectures, when dwelling on particular countries,

countries, with accounts of their remarkable state-revolutions, battles, curiosities, and natural productions; so while these juvenile astronomers are exhibiting, in miniature, the motions and aspects of the celestial wonders, on the Globe and Orrery, they should be informed of the most probable hypotheses and conjectures of the best astronomers.

When some advances have been made in historical reading, a regard ought to be had to method and chronological order, that young learners may be enabled to form correct ideas of the certainty of particular æras and epochs of time—to calculate, from the best authorities, the

length

length and duration of any interval of time; and, by comparing the computation of various ages and kingdoms, not only adjust the date of their respective transactions to some fixed period, but also determine the order and the succession of past events. It is from perusing the lives of departed excellence, and conversing with good and illustrious characters, that the soul seems to have enjoyed a pre-existence, and to catch an emanation of their virtues.

Such studies kindle, in the generous bosom of youth, a glow of emulative ardour, and animate to actions, which the future records of history will not blush to to hand down to the examination, and the approving eye of posterity.

The pages of history, likewise, hold out to our admiration and judgment those characters and examples among illustrious women, whose dignity of station, heroic and amiable virtues, will transmit their memory and names to the utmost extent of time.

They also discover those predominant views, dispositions and passions, of the human mind, which have, in a particular manner, supplied historic records with events; such as, having prevailed in an extraordinary degree, have led to transactions that have proved most fatal to the

the happiness of private individuals and families, or to the tranquillity and prosperity of kingdoms and empires.

Pre-eminent in this rank stand Pride and Ambition: the constituent parts of these baneful qualities are the love and practice of flattery, falsehood, treachery, dissimulation—with all the base accompanying arts of circumvention, and acts of cruelty.

The breast that is agitated by these passions is a stranger to the blessings of peace. Its insatiable desires are for ever pointing to something unpossessed, that mocks enjoyment; destroy the vital springs of happiness, and, from unceasing disap-

disappointments and mortifications, fail not to produce the keenest punishment to their possessor.

In the female breast, the force and power of those passions are more dangerous, when the inordinate love of fashionable attire, of gay and splendid amusements, mislead the senses, and, gaining an intire conquest over the mind, precipitate innumerable victims from honor, reputation, and happiness.

Pride and Ambition are tyrants which, usurping the dominion of the breast, either extinguish, or bind all other affections and passions in servile subjection. Even the barriers of honesty itself have been found

found insecure against their strong invasions. They close the mind upon the tenderest affections, repel friendship, reject conviction, and are composed of those properties on which reason cannot act.

I am, &c.

LETTER X.

SIR, *London, Jan. — 1803.*

As the intention of proving that the natural intellectual capacity of females is in every respect equal to those studies which have been more generally appropriated to the use of the opposite sex, has been uniformly the object of the preceding Letters, it is to be hoped, that the lordly monopolizers of knowledge will not think their privileges encroached upon, if the most useful

useful branches of natural and experimental philosophy be recommended to the notice of the Ladies.

In its present improved state, the elements of this science are brought down, with perspicuity, by many able writers, to the comprehension of the plainest capacity.

A little attention to this study will prepare the mind to behold, without ignorant wonder, the less common appearances and accidents of Nature. By an acquaintance with her laws and operations, we are certainly better enabled to understand, and to apply the various treasures that compose the vast magazine of her bounty, as well as to add to our own happiness and comfort, by a sensible enjoyment of them.

Great, likewise, are the religious advantages which arise from these august and comprehensive studies. They enlarge the capacities of the mind; they impress juster and more rational ideas of that Omnipotent Being, whose power commanded those respective wonders into existence; they give strength and purity to religious sentiments, by harmonizing with the beneficent doctrines of Christianity, whose benign and diffusive influence ends only with the utmost extent of created beings; they co-operate

operate with these doctrines in correcting the erring heart, and in perfectioning the human mind—and, as a stronger incentive, a true relish for the beauties of Nature is the most easy preparation, and gentlest transition, to an enjoyment of those of heaven.

But, however interesting and advantageous these subjects may be found in investigation; and, however essential they may be considered in an enlarged and intelligent plan of instruction, as supplying the ever-active, the ever-inquisitive mind with new and rational delight: they are not to exclude, or supersede, an earnest cultivation of te better knowledge of religion, whom they are

are to attend as lovely and fair companions only.

The doctrines of Christianity are of the first importance to assist the defective state of human nature. They temper, and give a due balance to the mind in the gay and seductive hours of prosperity; they compose and soften its anguish in the dreary state of pain and adversity: and, by discovering to the one the short period of temporal enjoyments, and to the other a speedy and infinite reward for patient hope, they sustain each under their respective and different temptations.—Yet, necessary and efficacious as these doctrines are, and excellent as are the precepts which they enjoin; they are rejected, in the modern schemes of education, for the study of History, and a variety of other literary compositions, of which the present times are so prolific. This fault has originated in the refinements of an age, that boasts of its superior polish.

When the mind has arrived at such a degree of independence as to feel its own strength sufficient, and to refuse the aid and authority of divine Revelation it must be considered as an alarming triumph of sentiment over religion; yet the superiority and necessity of Sacred Writ has been singularly manifested, by the fatal consequences

sequences that have arisen in the moral world, from a neglect of its use.

By some, indeed, the difficulty of the import of the Bible has been brought forward as an apology for its dismission: by others, that it contains certain passages which have a tendency to corrupt the morals, and are offensive to true delicacy. That Holy Writ exceeds the bounds of childish comprehension—that it is too sacred to afford merely exercises for reading, is certainly well determined. But, is there no period of youth to which the knowledge of this book may be adapted?

In order to reconcile these difficulties

and objections, selections are made of what are stiled the Beauties, or Purifications, of the Bible; compilations, which are distinguished for lively imagery, variety of incident, and superior language; such as render them altogether suitable to the age, pleasing and sacred novels.

Every canonical part of Scripture should be considered sacred; and we ought to lament, that some portion of so valuable a blessing has, from accidental causes, been withheld from us, rather than wish to diminish what Providence has graciously preserved, for our improvement, out of the wrecks and revolutions of ages. Whether

ther these Beauties or Extracts have not contributed to exclude the History whence they were taken, and whether they be not an impeachment of the rejected part, is at least questionable.

It would perhaps be better, if the study of the Bible were not undertaken by young people, until their reason had attained strength and solidity; and even then the assistance of clear and able commentaries is to be recommended. Those studies ought also to be conducted with method, beginning with the Old Testament, as containing the prophecies which foretold the events recorded in the New; and a history of the extraordinary dispensations

sations of Providence, which preceded the introduction of Christianity.

As to those passages by which the delicacy of some squeamish readers is wounded, their offensiveness derives its existence from the improper dispositions with which they are perused. One would, however, be induced to give a little more credit to those extremely delicate-minded and critical perusers of the Holy Scriptures, if one could only be convinced that other books, of an avowed pernicious tendency, were not sought after with avidity, and read with all the effect they were meant to produce. Over the sacred volumes also their eyes wander with unholy profa-

profanation, forgetting, while occupied with the letter, the immaculate spirit that dictated those divine ordinances.

They also forget, that these ordinances were written expressly to recommend and enforce the beauty and necessity of moral, as well as of corporeal, purity; that, by such observances, the peculiar dignity of the human character might be supported, and particularly distinguished. But let these refined critics decently throw a mantle over what their chaste eyes cannot behold without danger; and let it be done with silent reverence.

When pure Morality and Religion, unfettered by narrow prejudices, have united to form the female character, which is the basis on which that of all ranks should be raised: it is then that Rank and Fortune have a privilege of admitting the embellishments of ornamental parts, elegancies, or accomplishments, which have no higher claim than to be regarded as appendants only to the principal— Virtue—instead of being, as they are too often considered, the grand design.

It is through a proper medium, the result of just management, that the female mind is enabled to exhibit all the perfection of which human nature is capable. The lovely attributes that thence arise,

discover

discover their native powers and faculties; virtue and piety become so firmly established in their breast, that every action appears to be directed by their benign influence.

Even the precepts of Wisdom herself seem more attractive from the lips of a female, who possesses an intelligent and well-regulated mind. Such a woman appeals not to the passions for persuasion; she convinces the judgment by the purity of her actions and the solidity of her reasoning.

A regular exercise in, and a consciousness of Virtue, serve as a guard angelic—by which the presuming libertine is awed into respect

respect and distance.—Men of sense and honor approach an accomplished and virtuous woman as the companion of intellectual knowledge, as their counterpart.

The affections of her husband are inalienably her own: she is the maternal friend, the affectionate monitress of her children, whose youthful minds are inriched from the treasures of her own.

In her person are displayed the chastened adornments of elegance and taste. Her domestic arrangements, from the regularity of their system, appear to be conducted by invisible means. She performs the honors of hospitality with grace and dignity; to which the finest zest is given

given by her converse and smiles. She is moderate and discriminate in the choice of public amusements, and of society: regular, liberal, and sincere in acts of religion and benevolence. In solitude she experiences the pure gratifications arising from contemplative enjoyments: She finds every where a subject for moral exercises; intellectually aspiring to an intercourse with angels. Her thoughts are extended beyond the confines of corporeal existence, while she rejoices in the consideration of being engaged in a work, which prepares her for endless beatitude.

Yet, how great—how amiable—how exemplary soever, may be the virtues that adorn

adorn the humble and private rank of females, whom retirement, or unpropitious fortune has destined to the shades of obscurity; it is from exalted station only that female excellence can be fully illustrated. It is from the eminent heights of dignity and fortune that the brilliancy of example is able to attract surrounding admirers:— the examples of those distinguished females, who, rising superior to the corruption of the times, dare to be singularly good, endeavor to restore the Empire of Modesty, and have Courage to be Virtuous.

Thus, Sir, I close my attempt of tracing those lineaments of the female mind, which,

which, while they more strikingly exhibit the valuable and genuine properties of it, will, I hope, in some degree, serve to prove, that the imputed imperfections and defects of that sex, are contracted from example, or the effect of habit only, and are the offspring of neglect, or of improper tuition.

If any ideas, which have been suggested in the preceding Letters, be found capable of affording a hint to their advantage, either by the adoption of such practices as they recommend, or for the exercise of a more able pen, I shall sincerely rejoice.

I remain.

THE END.

J. ADLARD, Printer,
Duke-street, Smithfield.

www.ingramcontent.com/pod-product-compliance
Lightning Source LLC
LaVergne TN
LVHW061215060426
835507LV00016B/1942